What Is a
Forecast?

by Jennifer Boothroyd

Lerner Publications Company · Minneapolis

LERNER

SOURCE™

Expand learning beyond the printed book. Download free, complementary educational resources for this book from our website, www.lerneresource.com.

The images in this book are used with the permission of: © Handout/Getty Images, p. 4; © Bennet Barthelemy/Aurora/Getty Images, p. 5; NASA, p. 7; © Joe Raedle/Getty Images, p. 6, 8; Courtesy of the National Oceanic and Atmosphere Administration Central Library Photo Collection, p. 9, 11; © Jay Directo/AFP/Getty Images, p. 10; © iStockphoto.com/Paco Romero, p. 12; © dalmingo/ Shutterstock.com, p. 13; © VectorNM/Shutterstock.com, p. 15; © quavando/E+/Getty Images, p. 16; © iStockphoto.com/EdStock, p. 16; © iStockphoto.com/STEEX, p. 17; © digitalskillet/iStock/ Thinkstock, p. 18; © Catherine Yeulet/iStock/Thinkstock, p. 19; © Jupiterimages/Polka Dot/ Thinkstock, p. 20; © iStockphoto.com/kizilkayaphotos, p. 21; © iStockphoto.com/shalamov, p. 21.

Front Cover: Courtesy of the National Oceanic and Atmospheric Administration Central Library Photo Collection.

Main body text set in ITC Avant Garde Gothic Std Medium 21/25.
Typeface provided by Adobe Systems.

Lerner Publications Company
A division of Lerner Publishing Group, Inc.
241 First Avenue North
Minneapolis, MN 55401 USA

For reading levels and more information, look up this title at www.lernerbooks.com.

Library of Congress Cataloging-in-Publication Data

The Cataloging-in-Publication Data for *What Is a Forecast?* is on file at the Library of Congress.
 ISBN: 978–1–4677–3920–7 (LB)
 ISBN: 978–1–4677–4680–9 (EB)

Manufactured in the United States of America
1 – CG – 7/15/14

Table of Contents

Predicting Weather

Meteorologists are scientists. They study weather.

They use **data** to learn about weather. They get data from weather stations.

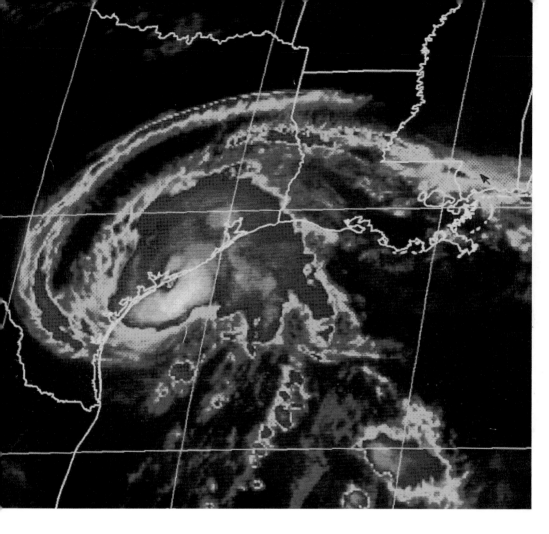

They get some data from
radar.

Satellites are
in space.

Satellites also send weather
data.

Meteorologists use computers.
They use maps and charts.

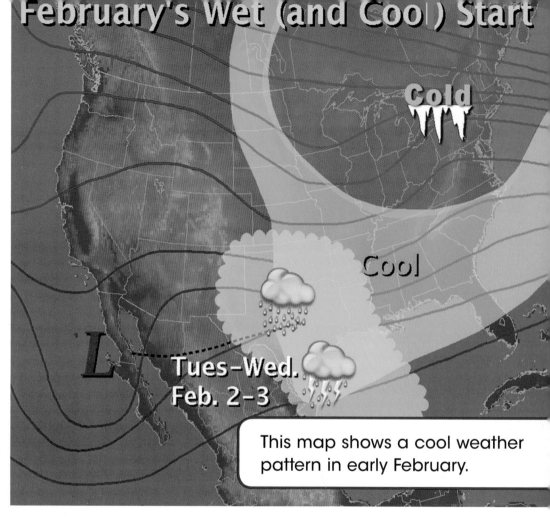

February's Wet (and Cool) Start

Cold

Cool

Tues–Wed.
Feb. 2–3

L

This map shows a cool weather pattern in early February.

They look for weather patterns.

Meteorologists **predict** what the weather will be.

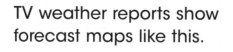

TV weather reports show forecast maps like this.

Weather predictions are called forecasts.

Forecasts Are Useful

What should I wear today?
I will check the forecast.

Denver   74°F | 23°C
May 24

Chance of Rain: 30%   UV Index: High
Wind: 13 mph   Sunrise: 5:49 am
Humidity: 51%   Moonphase:

Some forecasts show the weather for a day.

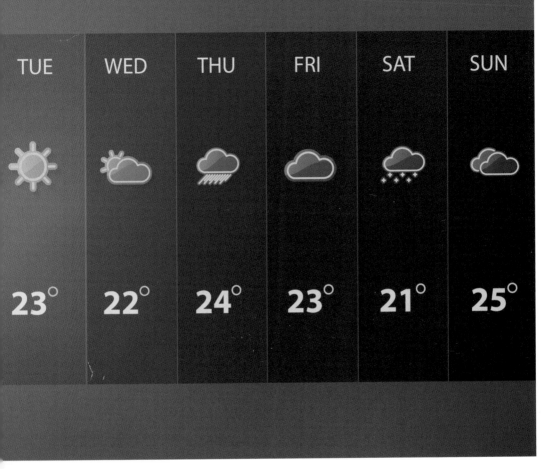

TUE	WED	THU	FRI	SAT	SUN
23°	22°	24°	23°	21°	25°

Other forecasts show the weather for a week.

The forecast predicted rain.

A forecast prepares people for the weather.

People prepare for
a hurricane.

A forecast warns people of
severe weather.

Weather can change quickly.

Forecasts are not always correct.

Forecasts help people make plans.

No one can be sure
what the weather will be.
18 Forecasts are good guesses.

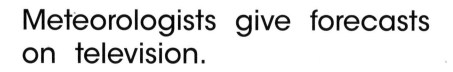

Meteorologists give forecasts on television.

Forecasts are read on the radio.

People use cell phones to find a forecast.

Weather forecasts help people stay safe and prepared.

Glossary

data – information

meteorologists – scientists who study weather

predict – to tell what might happen in the future

radar – a device used to track weather conditions

satellites – machines that orbit Earth to collect and send data

severe – very bad or likely to cause harm

Index